Copyright

Introduction

Color Basics: A Predictable Results Book

Color is at once fascinating and difficult. We look around and we see color combinations that are exciting, but then we have problems turning them into needlepoint. We want to feel more confident in our color choices, so we buy books, but then we end up frustrated because they are all about mixing paint. We see a lovely canvas but it's not quite right and we want to change one color. We do and the whole thing is so bad we abandon the project halfway through. We struggle to find a perfect background color but everything we pick feels wrong.

Have any of these things happened to you? They all have happened to us. In this Predictable Results book, and in several future books, we'll explore the topic of color in needlepoint. You'll learn:

- *A basic color vocabulary*
- *Why color in threads is different*
- *Basic color schemes and how to use them*
- *An easy way to create a color scheme*
- *How to check to see if your scheme "works"*

You can learn enough about color and how to use it so that you get reliable predictable results every time. Come follow us into what Walt Disney called "The Wonderful World of Color."

Color
Words & Wheels...

There are some basic words and concepts that are important to any discussion of color. Understanding what each means will make it much easier for you to develop color schemes, to understand why colors work together, and to adjust colors to suit your tastes.

Primary Colors are those colors that are not created by mixing two other colors. In fibers these are red, blue, and yellow. They are just like primary numbers which can't be divided by anything but themselves or 1. Primary colors can't be divided into other colors. Different media have different primaries (that's why the ink for your printer is yellow, magenta, and cyan).

Secondary Colors are made by mixing two adjacent primaries together. Red mixed with blue makes violet. Red mixed with yellow makes orange, and blue mixed with yellow makes green.

Tertiary Colors are those colors made by mixing a primary with a secondary. For example red mixed with orange makes red-orange. The conventions for naming these colors is to put the name of the primary first.

A color wheel made using these colors has twelve **hues** (the technical term for a color) arranged in a circle with yellow at the top. This is called the **Painter's Color Wheel** and will be the basis for our discussions. You might find it helpful to buy an inexpensive color wheel or color tool. An excellent choice is K1C2's Rainbow Color Wheel, available at art supply shops, knitting shops, and many craft stores. There are many other types of color wheels and color systems, but this is the most straightforward.

Any other color you see is some variation of these twelve basic hues, no matter what it is called. Color names, even more than colors themselves, are very subjective. What might be "pumpkin" to one stitcher, might be "persimmon" to another. For us as stitchers this is important because names often get reused but don't always name colors that are alike or even similar. In order to be accurate when specifying threads be sure to give the manufacturer, thread type, color name, and number (you may not have all this information, but capture as much as you can) when looking for color matches. If you and your shop "speak DMC" to each other, you can say "I need a silk to match DMC 666," and be reasonably sure you will get a bright, slightly orangish, red.

In addition to these 12 colors, there are three important **Neutral** colors that are used to create shades of the main hues. These are white, black, and neutral gray. In creating color schemes "neutral" has a broader definition we'll discuss on page 31.

Let's take a small detour here and explain why white and black can be added to any color scheme and not change it. Remember your science classes and learning about colors and light? Black is the absence of all colors, while white is the presence of all colors. In truth this is highly simplified, but it does explain what effect these colors have on color schemes. Like Type O Blood, black and white are universals. They go with any color without changing the color scheme. As a result, you can add white, black, or neutral gray to any color scheme and it remains the same.

That's good because otherwise you'd be limiting yourself, especially when it comes to backgrounds, and that would be challenging.

Tints are created when you mix white with a hue. These create colors that are lighter than the pure hue and are what we normally think of as "pastels."

Shades are created when you add black to a color. In non-technical terms we also use the word "shade" to refer to the many different versions of a color.

Tones are created in two ways, either by adding gray to a hue or by adding some of the complement to the hue. Tones created by adding the complement are often called **complementary tones.**

Value is the lightness or darkness of a color. Value is a continuum from white (high value) through black (low value) passing through many shades of gray. Typically the **value scale** used in color has ten values in it with black as 1 and white as 10.

On the last page of this book, 36, is a **value scale.** Print it out, paste it on some card stock or thin cardboard and punch a hole in each value. Number the values from 1 (black) to 10 (white). You now have a handy tool to find the value of any thread or patch of color.

To find the approximate value of a thread, place the value scale over the thread, then move it along until the value of the thread most closely matches the value on the card. Often you can't decide between two values. If that is the case, squint. This removes much of the "color" and leaves the value. When you almost can't see the difference between thread and scale – that's the right value.

We'll talk more about values and why they are important in the section on contrasts in color, page 8.

Colors also have *temperature.* This technical term also has a basis in how colors make us feel. We associate the cool colors of blue and violet with ice, the sky, and cool things. We associate the warm colors of yellow and orange with hot things like fire or the sun. Red and green are often considered "temperature neutral" because they can be either cool or warm based on their shade, their undertones, and their context.

Warm   Cool

Although everyone "knows" that red is a warm color, there can be "cool" reds. These are reds with some violet in them. For the colors at each end of the temperature groups, there can be versions of the color that feel like the other temperature. As an example think of a citrusy color scheme of orange, yellow, and yellow-green. Do you think of it as cool or warm? Many people think of it as warm, even though the yellow-green would, if paired with green and blue-green, feel cool.

Gray also has a temperature. **Warm grays** have a bit of yellow or orange in them. **Cool grays** have a bit of blue or violet. **Neutral grays** are just mixtures of black and white. You can figure out what type of gray you have by putting together a yellow swatch or thread, a blue swatch or thread, and your gray. Neutral grays will look cool next to the yellow and warm next to the blue. Cool grays will look cool next to both the blue and the yellow. Warm grays will look warm next to both the blue and the yellow. **Warm grays** are black, white, and a warm color, such as orange, yellow, or brown. **Cool grays** are black, white, and a cool color, such as blue or violet.

Intensity or *Saturation* is the most difficult color concept to understand. It refers to the brightness or dullness of a color. By convention, pure hues are also fully saturated (high saturation). Less saturated colors look muddy. The duller the color, the lower the saturation. You can have colors with high saturation that are tints and shades. This is why the concept is confusing; it doesn't relate directly to things like hue or value.

Unlike value, which is measurable, intensity is highly influenced by its surroundings. You only see the saturation of a color when you compare it to another color. It's easy to see this in action. Think of a sky blue. If you put it next to a pure blue, it's going to look a little subdued and a bit muddy. That's because sky blue is less saurated than pure blue, Put the same color next to black and it pops out, looking fully saturated. That's because black is less saturated than sky blue.

Color & Fiber

Has your love affair with color been one sided when stitching? Are you ever frustrated that you cannot find just the right color for a particular part of your canvas? Or noticed that not all ready-made colors of threads in the same hue (color) go together? Take greens for example. Some have dark undertones and others have more blue or yellow in them. When you put some darker greens with lighter greens that don't have the same color undertones they can appear odd as if they are not working together. Sometimes on a painted canvas the artist or designer did combine greens with different undertones intentionally.

Threads, fabrics, and fibers are different than paint. Paint is an example of a color that can be almost infinitely mixed to create new colors. If you're a painter, learning to mix colors comes with the territory.

Thread and fabric are examples of **discrete color**. There may hundreds of colors in one thread, but they are discrete and not continuous as is the case with paint. If you've ever looked at a color family of threads you have seen this. There are clear jumps between the shades in a family. While you do have a progression of values, it isn't continuous as it would be in paint.

You can "mix" colors in threads, however. Generally this is done by your eye in a process called **optical blending** (covered in the future book ***Shading Needlepoint***).

Most of the time though we deal with the colors that come to us in our threads.

With discrete colors you learn to manipulate color as it is available to you. You can only modify it by visual tricks. That means you may have to look further afield for the "right" color to a different thread, a different brand, a different technique, or a different stitch. All these ways to manipulate your needlepoint will be covered in future books.

If you've studied color before then you know the book has left out a third type of color, color in light or additive color. There the primary colors are different, the method of mixing is different, and even the role of black and white is different. This type of color is beyond the scope of our study. Books on this type of color will be less helpful for you as a stitcher.

Contrasts in Color

We may not consciously think about it, but contrasts define much of what we see and what we think of as beautiful. In the picture below left we see one petal overlapping another but how is this done?

English Roses, Anne Harwell, Canvas from Art Needlepoint.

Eiffel Tower, Georges Seurat, Canvas from Art Needlepoint.

It is done by creating the difference between the lighter edge of the top petal and the darker shadow of the petal below it. This creates a **contrast in value** that defines the shape of the flower.

Look at the picture above right. The contrast here is between the low intensity colors of the Eiffel Tower and the more pure colors of the sky. This gives the painting a **contrast in intensity.**

Ladies in Snow, Hiroshige, Canvas from Art Needlepoint.

There also can be **contrast in hue.** Many color schemes rely on the contrasting power of neutral vs. colors, complementary colors, or other color schemes to accent the focal point of the picture. In this woodblock above our eyes are drawn to the two ladies, partly because of the strong contrast between their colorful kimonos and the neutral background.

Many Flowered Tree, Renie Britenbacher, Canvas from Art Needlepoint.

Finally look at these amazing flowers and trees. Most of the colors here are intense, but there is still contrast. The sky and hills are big blocks of cool color, while most of the fowers have warm colors in them, creating a **contrast in temperature.**

Striped Kitty, Sophie Harding, Canvas from Art Needlepoint.

Most works of art have more than one kind of contrast, but contrast must be there to create a harmonious whole. Without contrast our work looks dull, flat, and undefined.

You can learn how to recognize contrast by looking at your stash of stitched and unstitched projects. Pick one at random. What contrasts are there? Are they strong? Do they lead you to the focal point?

Let's see this in action by looking at this painting by Sophie Harding. You can see the stitched version on the cover.

- ***Is there a contrast in value?*** *Only a little bit. There are touches of black and white and slightly different values in orange and green, but mostly it's a narrow range of values.*

- ***Is there contrast in intensity?*** *No, most of these colors are highly saturated.*

- ***Is there contrast in temperature?*** *Yes, the warm cat contrasts nicely with the cool background. There are no cool colors in the cat and no warm colors in the background.*

- ***Is there contrast in color?*** *Almost, the main colors are orange and green, not complements but near complements. This color scheme, discussed on page 27, can be so powerful it almost vibrates.*

With any canvas you have, stitched or unstitched, you can ask yourself these questions to understand more about the canvas and why it works.

Contrast

Using contrast effectively is so important to making your needlepoint look good that it can make or break a piece. In this section we'll look at two unstitched vintage pieces from Janet's stash, one with poor and one with good color contrast. Both are analyzed.

Vintage mini-sock, Canvas from Needlepoint, Inc.

This piece has been in her stash for several years. She loves the design but the colors have kept her from stitching it. There is lots going on here. There are many motifs, most of them about the same size. But the real problem is color. Seven colors are used: white, red, dark green, yellow, pink, black, and aqua. One color, white, is clearly the background color. Two colors,

aqua and black, are used sparingly so they are accents.

The other four (red, yellow, pink, and dark green) are used in about equal amounts. That means there is not a contrast of extent (see page 20 to see a design analyzed for this). One color should be used more than the others to create this kind of contrast.

A second problem is the lack of value contrast. You can see how value contrast makes a difference by looking at the flower ribbon on the right. This has dark green leaves, medium-light (but saturated) pink flowers, and a lighter pastel yellow border. It makes more sense than the heart border at the top where similar values make it so you don't know where to look. Nothing tells you what is different or important.

The most critical problem is that these four colors plus the aqua accent are all bright. Even the dark green, which could easily be lower saturation, is bright. The contrast that might be here disappears in all these bright colors. If some colors were more pastel, some muted, and some bright, you'd get contrast in intesity and the design wouldn't look confused. Doing this would also fix the value problem.

When contrast is missing or minimal in a piece, the viewer gets confused. There is no way to rank what is important and what is less important. Figures melt into backgrounds, and backgrounds can look like focal points. Your eyes jump from place to place in the picture, never resting. What could be lovely becomes confused.

This piece (pictured at right), a vintage design from dede's Needleworks, has much better understanding of color theory. This simple design of interlocking ribbons shows much better contrast. There are two ribbons, a blue one that is an endless knot and a multi-colored one.

Let's look at each ribbon individually. The blue ribbon has several different values of the same blue. While they are all pretty saturated, the value range is large. Clearly blue is the dominant color in this piece.

The multi-colored ribbon has lime, aqua, pale yellow, lavender, and pink in it. The value range here is much narrower (all are high values), but there is a contrast in intensity. This ranges from the very saturated aqua to the muted lime and washed out pale yellow.

Celtic knot, Canvas from dede's Needleworks

As a result you have a balanced piece with contrast in extent, value, and intensity. It will be a fun piece to stitch.

Contrast in value, while the easiest to do, doesn't have to be the only way color contrasts in your piece; other types of contrast can make effective design. In some color schemes, especially monochromatic and analogous, there isn't lots of contrast inherant in the scheme. To create an exciting piece of needlepoint, you'll have consider other ways to increase contrast.

Remember, when you are doing something like this to rank your threads and stitches (covered in an upcoming book) according to which attracts the most attention:

- **More saturated colors over grayed out colors**
- **Shiny threads over matte ones**
- **Furry threads over smooth ones.**
- **Metallic threads over shiny.**
- **High stitches over low stitches.**
- **Stitches with full coverage over open stitches.**

Always try to match stitches, threads, and colors that will attract attention to the areas in your canvas you want to emphasize. If you want all the attention to be on the center of a sunflower, pick the most attention-getting thread, color, and stitch for it. If you want to emphasize the petals instead make the center's color duller and use smooth, matte threads in a low stitch.

You could use contrast of intensity, combining bright, fully saturated hues with muted hues. Just put the brights on the focal point.

You could use contrast in texture, combining similar values with contrasting textures.

Depending on your design, you could combine contrast in value with contrasting shapes. Think of large vs. small, square vs. round, or many vs. few.

Applying Contrast to Painted Canvases

Even when we stitch a painted canvas, we can use the principles of color and contrast to create great needlepoint. Let's do this by looking at the mini sock and seeing how we can correct it.

Color: Change out one or two colors by changing their value and/or intensity. This adds contrast and makes the piece make sense. If you made the green darker, the yellow paler, and the pink slightly grayed, the increased value range would put the emphasis on red because it is the only pure hue. Yellow becomes another background color, and green and pink become the major accents.

Extent: There isn't any reason why all the green should be one shade. That would change the balance of color in the piece. Some areas of green are background, some are accents, and some are the focal point of the motif. What if three greens were used, making the darkest the background areas, the middle the accents, and the brightest, the focal points? That would make green seem smaller in extent than red.

Vintage mini-sock, Canvas from Needlepoint, Inc.

Combined with yellow as background, the color emphasis is on red and pink.

We'll come back to this canvas in a later book to talk about picking stitches for it.

The Main Color Schemes

There are color combinations we find pleasing and these form the basis of the main types of color schemes. These combinations of color show up everywhere – fabrics, advertisments, art, house colors, and packaging.

Knowing and understanding each of these schemes will allow us to create better-looking needlepoint, and allow us to create original projects that look good.

The basic color schemes all come from the color wheel discussed on page 4. The relation of one color to another on the wheel determines the color scheme. In the following sections we'll discuss six of the most common. Then we'll cover a simple way to create your own color schemes.

Monochrome

It's easy to figure out what this scheme is from the word: "mono" meaning "one" + "chrome" meaning "color." So a monochrome color scheme is one that uses a single color.

The simplest monochromatic color scheme would be a single color. A common type of this scheme would be a card of paint chips. There the color is the same but the value is different, shading from light to dark.

We're lucky as stitchers because our threads are often already arranged for us into monochromatic color schemes, but we don't think of them that way. We call them color families. In any thread a color family will be a range of values of the same color. Thread color families can have anywhere from 2 to 8 shades in them.

If you want to make a very easy monochromatic color scheme just pick a single color family of thread. Add white or black as the background and you'll have a perfectly coordinated palette.

Putting together a color scheme with a single color family produces lovely results.

It's also simple to do. We may also find that we need to create a color scheme using more than one thread.

Sometimes there aren't enough shades in the color family to stitch the design. Sometimes there is a larger gap between two of the shades, so you need another thread to fill in. Sometimes you are stitching from stash and can only get a range of colors with a variety of threads.

To create a monochrome color scheme of your own, begin with a single color family of thread. Look at those colors together. Then analyze it by asking yourself these questions:

- ***Do you need more threads at either the light or dark end?*** *Pick those first.*

- ***Do you want to substitute other threads for any of the shades in your initial family?*** *Pick those now.*

- ***Squint at the initial color family. Does there seem to be more space between some colors than others?*** *Look for threads to fill those gaps.*

- ***Finally, pick any other threads that look similar to the initial family, even if they are "the same" as your initial threads. A key to finding good color combinations is pulling more threads than you need, so that you can pick the best combination.***

Pull at least twice as many threads as you need, and keep them in the project bag in case one of the threads picked doesn't work out.

Once you have all the prospective threads, line them up from light to dark. Do any of them stand out as being not quite the same color as the others? Let's say the color wanted is true greens. Some of the threads picked might too olive (yellow-green) or too teal (blue-green) when you put your initial choices in a pile. Discard these immediately.

Repeat the process squinting a bit. Squinting will remove some of the color information. If you squint enough, you will only see value, which is important in other contexts, but not here. Once again pull threads that are too different and that stand out from the other threads.

Now you should be left with a range of colors that appear to be in the same color family. It's time to take a moment to think about texture.

Texture is an important aspect in needlepoint because it is an important aspect of thread. In monochromatic color schemes, texture can be one of your best friends. Texture allows the "same" color to look different. This is because texture allows light to reflect off the thread differently. By using different textures you

White Bargello Jewelry Box, Design from Janet M. Perry

can easily expand the threads in your color scheme.

You can see this in practice by picking several threads the same color in your stash. You might have three very similar greens – DMC pearl cotton, Sparkle Rays, and Soft Sheen Fyre Werks. Because there is an increasing amount of metallic in the three threads, they "look" progressively lighter. In a group of threads there are shiny threads, metallics, metallic blends, matte threads, and perle cottons. All work together because they are the same color, but they add some additional contrast that is important in monochromatic schemes.

The key to any good design is contrast. Because monochrome schemes by their nature don't have contrast in hue, the other kinds of contrast, especially value, become more important. By pushing to find a wider range of values and different textures, monochrome pieces can be very exciting.

Complementary

The easiest way to describe a complementary color scheme is that they are colors across from each other on the color wheel.

As a result, complements are pairs, such as:

- **Red & green**
- **Yellow & violet**
- **Blue & orange**

Every color has a complement to it. In each of these pairs there is one primary color and one secondary color. Each of the secondary colors is made up of the other two primary colors. Let's break them down:

- **Red (primary) has green (blue + yellow) as the complement**
- **Yellow (primary) has violet (blue + red) as the complement**
- **Blue (primary) has orange (red + yellow) as the complement**

So in these pairs of complementary colors you have a sense of "completeness" because all the primary colors are in the pairs.

With the addition of a second color, we have lots more to use in making our palette. Now there are all the different shades of each color in the complement pairs, as well as black, white, and neutral gray.

Adding all these shades gives wonderful variety. Think of a floral canvas of many shades of pink flowers with dark green leaves. You can almost see all the variety that comes from the contrast of red and green.

Holly, Canvas from Whimsy & grace

Look at this piece from Whimsy & grace (pictured above), the complementary colors of red and green are the only colors used. Notice how the green dominates with different shades for each leaf and two values of each shade. The simpler red berries are a great accent. The piece shows how great a color scheme complementary colors can be.

A complementary pair inherently has contrast in it, as we saw. How do we take that and extend it into a working set of colors and threads?

Begin by looking at the design at right, and think about where the colors would be placed. The example design is a stained glass pattern from Dover. This will be the line drawing for a needlepoint piece.

There are three open poppies, three buds, some stems and a background. The open poppies are the focal point and they will be red. The tops of the poppy buds will be red as well but the stems and the bottoms of the buds will be green.

Clearly red is dominant here, so use neutrals for the background, maybe a pale

gray in different threads. That would look like a cloudy sky. Happily, poppies have black centers, a neutral color, making the poppies even more of a focal point because of the strong value contrast between the black centers and the pale gray background. So the colors are a complementary scheme: red flowers with black centers and green stems on a neutral gray background.

Make the design more complex without changing the color scheme by using shading in the petals of the open poppies.

Without picking stitches or threads what contrasts are here?

- ***Contrast in extent*** – *there is far more red than green in this design.*
- ***Contrast in value*** – *pale gray background and black centers*
- ***Contrast in color*** – *red and green with no other colors*
- ***Contrast in complexity*** – *shades of red, fewer shades of green*

Nothing here is unrealistic, but it is the start of a good strong design. The next step in making this needlepoint is to translate the areas into threads. This could be simple, threads of all one type, or complex with threads that have contrasts in texture (wool for the stems, silk for the flowers, something nubby for the centers).

Now that we've got threads, can our stitches add more to this design? Some areas, such as the stems, are narrow and will be best done in Tent. But what about the background or the flowers? Other stitches might add even more texture to this.

The design itself, when colored, has plenty in it to make it great without using more than one thread or stitch. But if you think about the design and how your choice of thread and stitches can change things, you can get something even better.

> **For any potential design that uses a complementary color scheme, remember to look for contrasts to create an effective design. If the colors are balanced in this way, your thread and stitch choices only make the finished piece better**.

Creating good complementary designs is easier than for many other color schemes because the basis of good design is built into the color pairs – you just need to enhance it. If you are uncertain about color in your needlework, choosing this scheme is a good place to start.

Analogous

The easiest way to describe an analogous color scheme is that they are made of colors next to each other on the color wheel. This color scheme can incorporate as few as two colors or as many as five or more. In these schemes all the colors are found together on the color wheel.

That makes this scheme kind of like a gradation; there are many commonalities between any two colors next to each other, but fewer between the colors at either end of the scheme.

It's this commonality that makes analogous schemes calming. They have less contrast in many ways than any other color scheme but monochrome. Often the result is very calm and subtle, and because the colors share a primary to some extent, the contrasts are subdued. The bellpull, next page left, uses bright colors in many analogous combinations.

Here too, in spite of the bright colors, the feeling is calm.

Putting together an analogous scheme with solid threads is pretty easy. The project pictured on the next page right, is a quilt block stitched in an analogous scheme. This will be used as an example of how to develop this color scheme.

Begin by selecting a solid-colored thread (we'll deal with overdyes in the section on creating a color scheme on page 34). Find where it is on the color wheel. Blue-violet is used in the example. The touchstone color is found in the upper left rectangle.

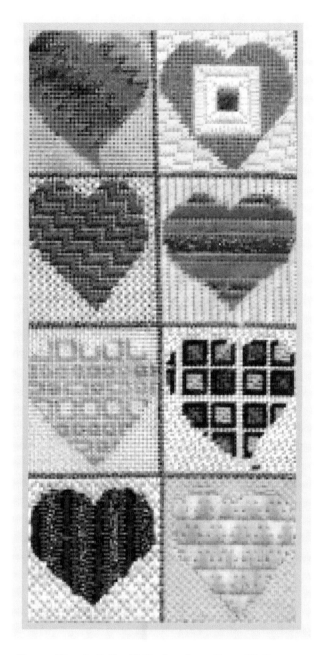

Happy Hearts Bellpull, Design from Janet M. Perry

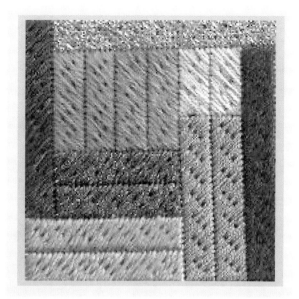

Asymmetrical Log Cabin Quilt Block, Design from Janet M. Perry

Next think about the value of the color. Is it light, dark or in the middle? Now you know the color and the value. It's a medium shade on the darker side.

If you have a project in mind, look at it now. How many different colors (including shades) will you need? In this project there are nine colors. It's designed with four colors with two shades of each color. That left one block not allocated. Looking at this design, each color gets about the same treatment, so there isn't be a clear dominant color. The extra block was given to a color used slightly less (blue), but any of the colors could be chosen in this particular design.

There will be four colors in the design. The next step is to decide where in the continuous series these additional colors will be found. One way is to add in the colors on either side of the touchstone color, blue-violet, putting in blue and violet. That makes three colors.

The next question is whether the fourth color will be red-violet or blue-green. The one will have violet dominant; the other will have blue dominant. Unless other evidence (such as the other colors in a room, the taste of the intended recipient, etc.), this is where thread selection come into play.

Begin by picking threads in the colors already chosen. Put them together. "Test drive" the possible choices by picking out threads in one of the color possibilities. For this project, you need two shades. Do you have two you like? If not, go to the other color. If so, lay them with the other threads.

Lay the new threads aside and repeat the process with the other color. Then decide which you like better and add them to your pile of threads.

If, as was the case in this project, you have extra areas look at the colors you have picked. Does one of those colors seem to be prominant? You could pick that color for your extra to make it more dominant, or you could pick a color which seems to be used less to balance the colors. As in many things with color, your needs and taste determine the result.

Because you have started with a single color and built out your analogous scheme step-by-step from that point, you have a combination of threads and colors that works. This same step-by-step process can be used to create any color scheme.

To create an analogous scheme:

- *pick a touchstone color*

- *add the colors on either side*

- *assign these colors to the areas in your design*

- *if more hues are needed, use other clues to pick which adjacent color to add*

- *if needed add in black, white, and neutral gray*

- *substitute or add more threads in the same colors*

Split Complement

While split complement schemes are easy to explain, they can be the most challenging color schemes of all to use.

A split complement uses a group of three analogous colors, usually a primary or secondary, and the colors on either side of it. Then it adds the complement of the middle shade and then drops that middle color of the original three out.

You can also create a valid, though less common, split complement scheme, by NOT dropping out the middle color. Only one book on color, **Color Choice** by Stephen Quiller, explains Split Complements this way. When you find this combination in other books, it is often called an Analogous Complement.

There are other types of split complement that are more complex. A common one uses two complementary groups of analogous colors and may drop the middles out of both.

This is often called a Double Split Complement.

No matter which scheme you are using, split complements are more challenging to create than other color schemes. At least in part this is because there are so many colors to handle. This is true of all color schemes: the more colors in the scheme, the harder it is to find a harmonious group of colors.

There are a couple of reasons for this. First, the more colors you have the more chance there is for unharmonious interactions to occur because many colors aren't true, causing some elements in the colors not to work well together. Second, when working with any material, you might be limited in the selection for a particular color. When this happens, it can skew a scheme with more colors making it hard to find enough other colors to work in that scheme. In threads, orange and violet have the most limited selection (though it is getting better). If your scheme has one of these hues, you may find it harder to get a good color scheme.

To construct a split complement scheme, begin with three analogous colors. You'll find it easiest if the trio you pick is a color and the tertiary colors on either side. So red-orange, orange, and yellow-orange is an easier basis for a split complement scheme than red, red-orange, and orange.

Pick the complement of the middle color. In this case, that would be blue. You have four colors: red-orange, orange, yellow-orange, and blue. At this point you can decide if you want to keep the middle analogous color in the mix or not.

But why does this scheme work? With or without the orange present, we "see" both red-orange and yellow-orange as shades of orange, not as shades of red or yellow. This happens because the complement of orange, blue, implies the presence of orange as the unifying theme in all the colors. Keep the orange in the mix and that theme is even stronger.

That's the power of the split complement.

Beginning with the more difficult set of analogous colors (red, red-orange, and orange), we add red-orange's complement, blue-green. In our analogous trio red-orange is the glue that holds the scheme together because it is a combination of red and orange. It is a unifying element but a less strong one than orange in the first scheme because it is not present in the other two colors, but a blend of them.

Drop out red-orange and the connection between the remaining three colors becomes subtler. This is the kind of split complement often seen in color books, which could be why this scheme is a difficult one for many folks. It can look contrived.

When creating a scheme with several colors, think about intensity and value. Unlike some of the simpler schemes where additional values or intensities just give you more choice, in split complement schemes they are needed to keep the piece from looking confused. Too many colors of equal value can look dull because there isn't enough contrast. Too many colors of equal intensity vibrate and are too exciting. It's contrast that makes the scheme harmonious.

The easiest way to do this with a color scheme is to identify the background hue, even if it is much darker or brighter than you would like. Now change the value and lower its intensity. If your scheme has several analogous hues, push them further apart to create more contrast: lighten one, darken another, change the intensity in a third. Immediately you create more contrast, making the scheme more effective.

Near Complement

This color scheme isn't one you're likely to find in most color books, but it's surprisingly common. To create a near complement scheme, begin with a pair of complements, then move one of the pair one color over. That's a near complement, we call it that because it is "near" the complement pair but not exact complements.

Some near complement pairs are:

- *Red & blue*
- *Green & violet*
- *Green & orange*
- *Yellow & blue*

And so on.

If a complement pair is blue and orange, two near complements would be yellow and blue, which moves one away from orange, and orange and green, which moves one away from blue.

Often people think some of these pairs don't "go" together or that the colors "clash." The less pejorative name of near complement conveys the better idea that not all color schemes of this type clash and helps demonstrate their popularity.

In a clash color scheme, two things need to be present. First, the colors need to be saturated and of equal intensity. Have you ever noticed that if you put two bright solid threads together that they vibrate? This happens when the colors are equal in intensity. The closer the colors are to complements, the more they vibrate. You can dilute this effect quickly by using neutrals. The second thing needed to make a clash is no neutrals.

Stars & Blocks Quilt Portrait, Design from Napa Needlepoint

This quilt portrait has a clash scheme of bright blue and bright red. It really vibrates because these two colors are of equal intensity and are next to each other often.

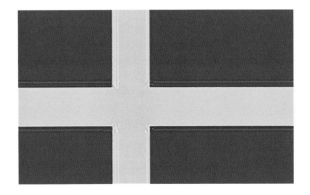

Swedish flag

Near complement pairs are a common color scheme in flags. Rarely do they clash because the colors are diluted by the white. Even a small amount of white will do. To see this in action, look at two very similar flags. Both the Swedish, pictured on the left, and Norwegian, pictured below, flags use near complement pairs; blue and yellow for Sweden and red and blue for Norway. Both flags use the same cross as well. The Swedish flag vibrates, especially near the cross, while the other flag does not.

Why?

Norwegian flag

In the Norwegian flag while the color pair is a near complement, there is white surrounding the blue cross. That provides a visual break preventing the clash.

Clash schemes are powerful color schemes that look very modern. They are best in small doses. They can be cool and effective schemes and quite addicting.

More intense colors work well to create clash schemes, but they are not the only possibilities for near complements. By controlling intensity, you can put two near complements together and avoid a clash. A classic outfit of jeans (blue but muted with darker blue and white because of the fabric) and a red T-shirt shows how well this works. Any red, even an intense one, works because the blue is subdued. That's a way to get a near complement scheme that doesn't vibrate.

Dilution is the key to making a near complement scheme work. This can be done in several ways.

One way, seen in the Norwegian flag, is to add white or another neutral. White works best because black tends to intensify colors, and should be avoided in this case.

Another way to dilute the color scheme is to lower the intensity of one or both colors. No one thinks baby blue and pastel pink clash because their intensity is low. By picking a light, less intense, version of one color in the pair as the background, you create a pleasing near complement scheme without using neutrals. Your choice of threads can aid in this. Soft threads, such as wool, look less intense than harder threads like cotton floss.

Start to construct this scheme by picking a complement pair. Decide which of the pair you want to change. Having done this,

Tumbleweed Quilt Block, Design from Janet M. Perry

decide which color on either side of the changed compliment you want to use. The quilt portrait, previous page, started with blue-orange. Orange was swapped out for red. In the quilt block pictured above, yellow was picked instead of orange. The intensity of this color was lowered and it made an effective background color.

Once you have picked your two colors, you need to ask yourself if you want clash or not? If you do, play around with your thread choices until you find a combination that vibrates when laid next to each other. Do not add other colors or even additional shades of these colors. Any addition will dilute the clash.

But what if you don't want a clash?

There are several things you can do:

- *Add more threads in one color. This puts stronger emphasis on one of the pair, changing the balance.*

- *Tone down one or both colors by using tints, tones, and shades.*

- *If you do this just be careful not to use more than one color that is muted and low intensity that is equal in value to another low intensity color. This combination creates something very, VERY dull.*

- *Add neutrals, white before black, to dilute the combination and act as a buffer.*

The further away from each other the colors are in value and intensity, the more pleasing the combination will be.

The design might also help you with this. In the quilt block pictured on page 29, the center pinwheel is clearly the focal point. By making the pinwheel blue and the rest of the quilt yellow, blue is clearly the dominant color. But what if blue and yellow alternated in the pinwheel on a white background? How would that have changed things?

Neutral

You may think you know what neutrals are, but, in fact, the definition of neutrals varies greatly depending on the context. There are at least three definitions that only partially overlap.

The strictest is the artist's definition. A neutral is a color with no temperature. That includes only white, black, and neutral gray. All other colors are combination of colors that have temperature and therefore are not neutral.

Everyone agrees that these are neutrals but other uses expand this definition.

In home décor, neutrals are these colors plus a whole range of light and dark browns and tans that "go with" anything. They are "neutral" in that they don't much affect the other colors in the room. There are even decorating books that expand this even more to huge ranges of muted colors, both light and dark, with lots of brown/tan in them, but this is wide open for discussion.

Janet saw this recently in her house. She isn't a neutral person and the tan "developer's special" carpet has not been replaced in her son's room. When turning this room into a sitting room on a budget, there wasn't money to replace the carpet. She bought some striped blue and oatmeal curtains at Target and that horrible carpet works with the blue and black in the room, simply because it is a neutral.

The widest definition of neutral comes in clothing. It encompasses the other neutrals but it adds some of its own. While navy blue is considered a neutral in clothing, it isn't neutral for anything else. Some people add even more colors such as dark violet, bright red, and olive green to the fashion neutrals. Fashion neutrals don't always adapt well as neutrals in needlepoint because viewers tend to see them as a hue not as a neutral.

The key thing for all neutrals is that neutral colors go with pretty much everything. When picking a neutral scheme for your needlepoint, think about the end use. A neutral pillow should be decorator's neutrals, but a purse could be fashion neutrals.

In needlework, gold and silver also function as neutrals. While metal jewelry is neutral in fashion, in decorating most professionals would think of metal as an accent and as a color of its own.

A big problem in making a neutral color scheme is blandness. All too often neutral not only means a limited range of color, but it becomes a limited range of values as well. As we've learned, contrast is needed to make a color scheme work, Neutral schemes often lack contrast.

Whenever you have contrast in a neutral color scheme, it needs to be enhanced. For example if the contrast is in value pick colors wide apart on the value scale.

If the contrast comes from texture, pick threads with big contrasts in texture. For example in an all-white piece go for not only a range of whites or creams, but add

a metallic. Also be sure that you include some matte threads (wool) some threads with some sheen (silk or pearl cotton) and maybe some shiny ribbons (Neon Rays); the piece will look better for it.

By pushing the contrasts, you'll have a piece where the design does not disappear.

Diamond Knot Variation Quilt Block, Design from Janet M. Perry

How does this work on a practical scale? Let's use the little patchwork block pictured above as an example. One color is used for the ribbon, one for the details, and one for the background.

Start with the ribbon color. Then go on to pick the detail thread. It should be different in color, texture, or both, from your ribbon thread. It might take several tries to get this right.

A dark gray, almost black, didn't have enough difference between it and the ribbon thread; it would all look like one color.

A light gray was a little too close to the white background. It might have worked, but something a bit darker would give more contrast. A warm gray was used, giving a little contrast in temperature, which, while tricky, can often work.

Follow the same process to construct neutral schemes for any piece. Pick your main "color" first. Then, thinking about contrasts, pick the accent colors from most to least used. This is where some threads that have an additional kind of contrast with the other threads can be used. Finally, pick a background color that continues the kind of contrast you are using but that harmonizes with the other colors.

Creating A Color Scheme Easily

As stitchers we are lucky because we have a readily available source of color schemes in overdyed threads. These threads come in many fibers, colors, and color schemes. They are an endlessly wonderful source of color ideas for your needlepoint.

An overdyed thread is a widely available source of color schemes of all kinds. Begin by untwisting the skein, if it's twisted. Twisting can change the balance of the colors. Now identify which of the main color schemes it uses. (Be warned some overdyes use a multi-color scheme, an issue we'll discuss in a later book.)

Once you know the color scheme, write down the non-neutrals in your skein. Because of the way these threads are made there are often many complementary tones, ignore these. Most overdyes have three colors in them, although some can have five or more.

One of the colors will be dominant and the other two will be accents. Note which is dominant.

Armed with this information, you're ready to create your color scheme. You have a project in mind. In the overdye are there enough colors for the project? If so, pick your threads to match the colors in the overdye and start to stitch.

If not, then you need to expand the color range. This can be done by adding different shades of the colors or by extending the color scheme, or both. If your scheme is analogous, you can extend the scheme and add shades. If your scheme is complementary you can only add shades. From these colors pick out threads. At this point you can decide if you want to include your overdye in your piece or not. If you don't, that's OK because it has allowed you to create a great color scheme.

Test Driving Color Schemes

Sometimes you just aren't sure about your scheme even if you have tested the threads in their packaging by pulling out the colors that don't fit your scheme.

Sometimes you just aren't sure where to place the colors in your design. This is especially true for geometrics. If we don't know, a good thing to do is stitch up some quick tests. Since Janet hates making needlepoint that can't be turned into something, she makes simple 8-pointed stars, pictured below, to test color schemes.

Make half the points one color and half the other. They are so small and quick to stitch you could make several, figuring out in advance how you want the colors to work.

If a test is wanted of three colors, use a larger star. The pictures below are color studies stitched as eight-point stars and finished as ornaments. An overdyed thread is used for the single color diamonds.

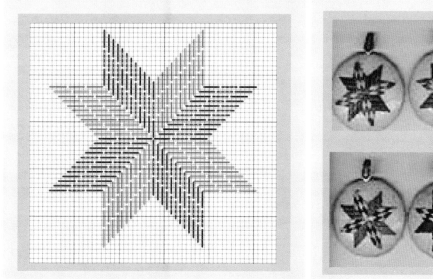 

Eight-point Star chart and color combinations, designed by Janet M Perry

Value Scale

Print out and paste it on some card stock or thin cardboard. Punch a hole in each value. Number the values from 1 (black) to 10 (white). You now have a handy tool to find the value of any thread or patch of color. To find the approximate value of a thread, place the value scale over the thread, then move it along until the value of the thread most closely matches the value on the card.

Made in the USA
San Bernardino, CA
13 June 2014